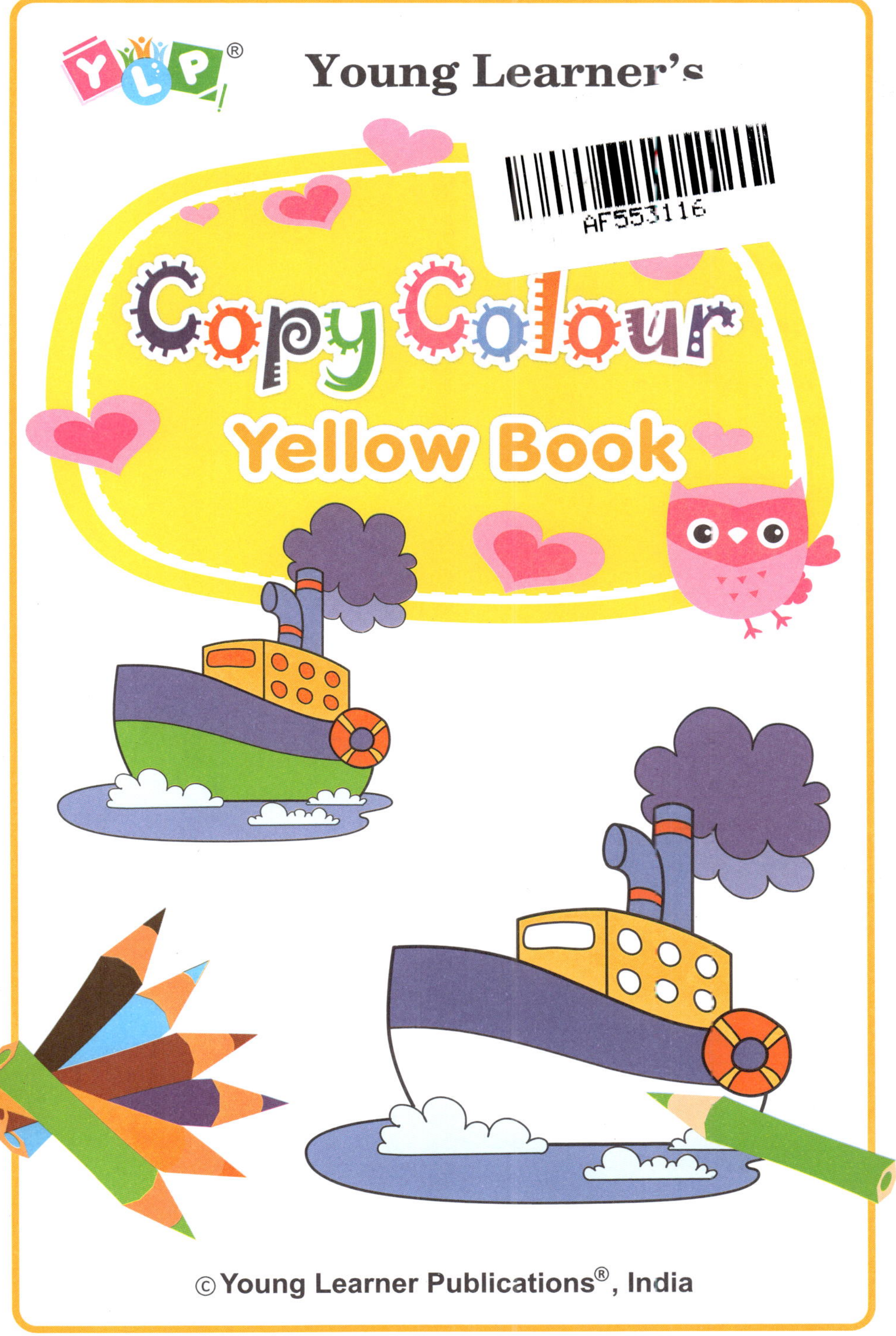
YLP
Young Learner's
Copy Colour
Yellow Book
AF553116
© Young Learner Publications®, India

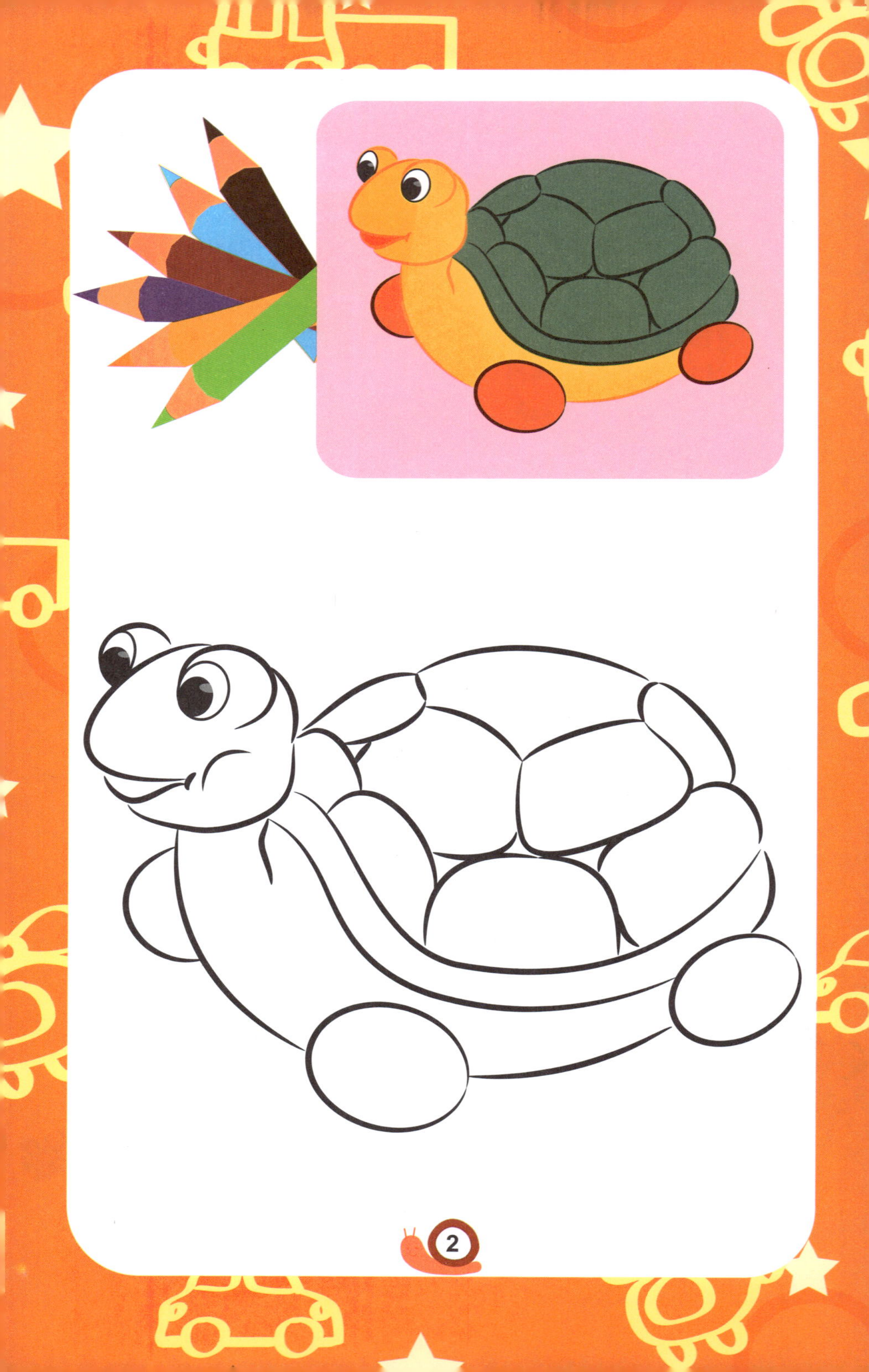

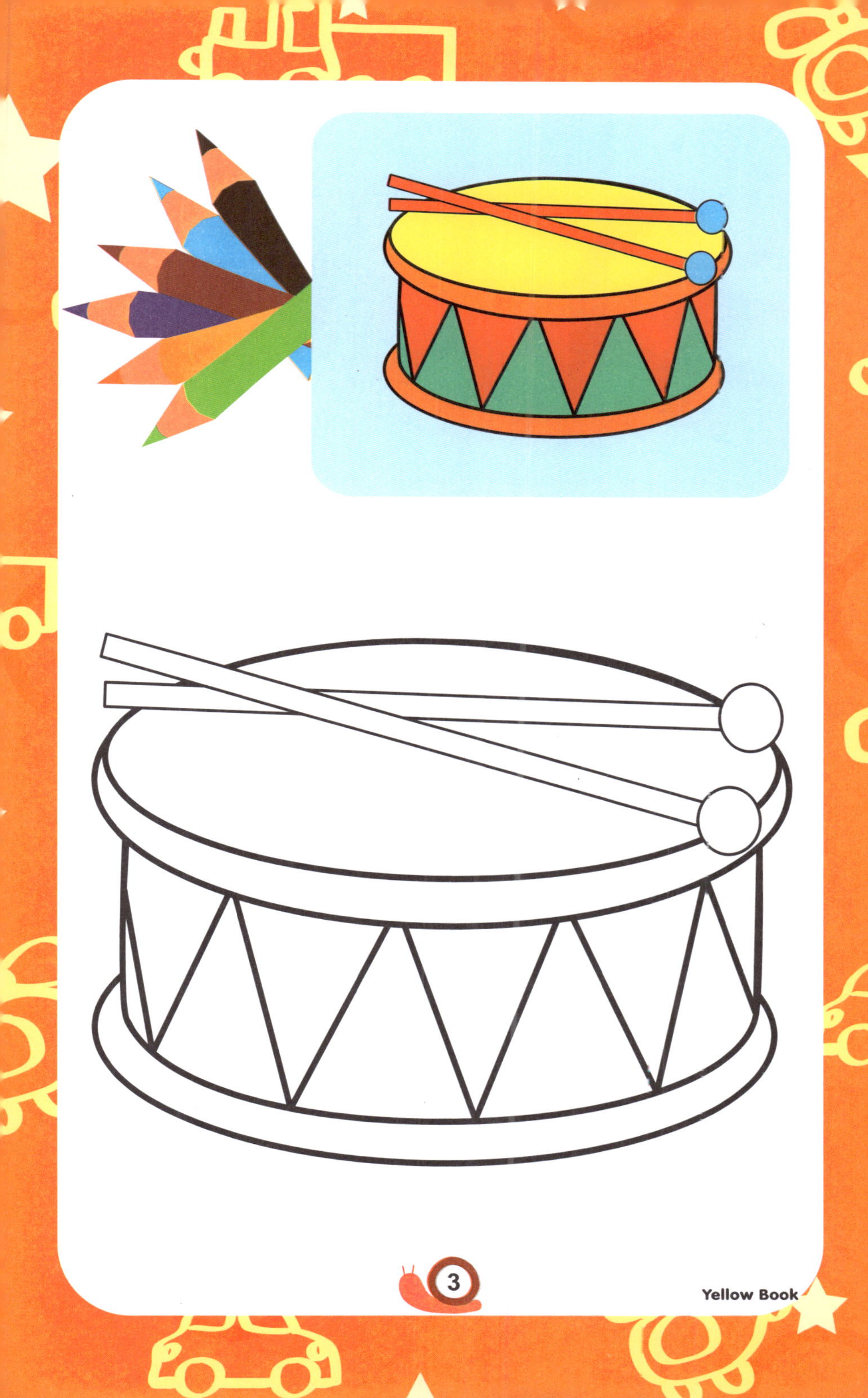

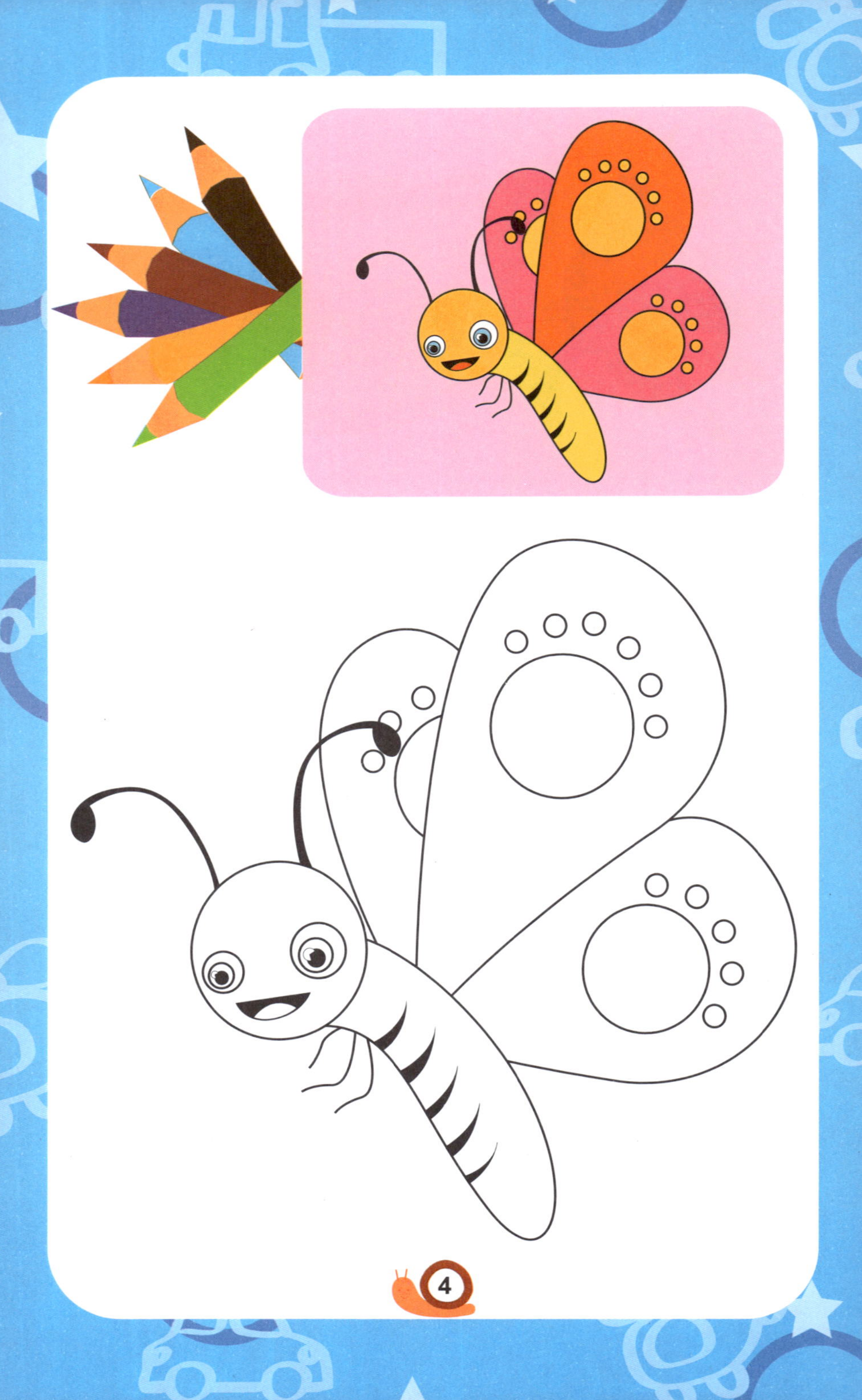

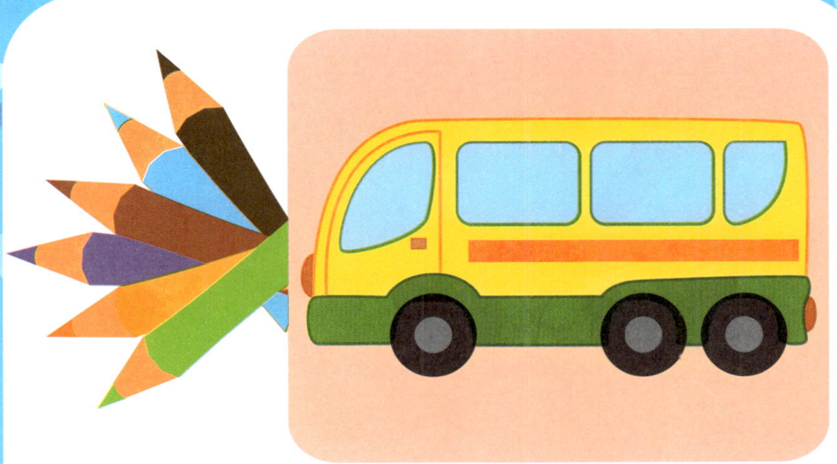

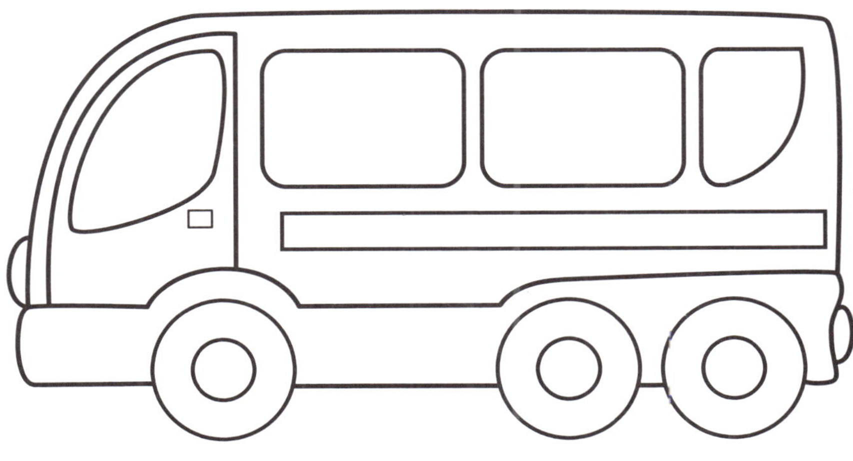

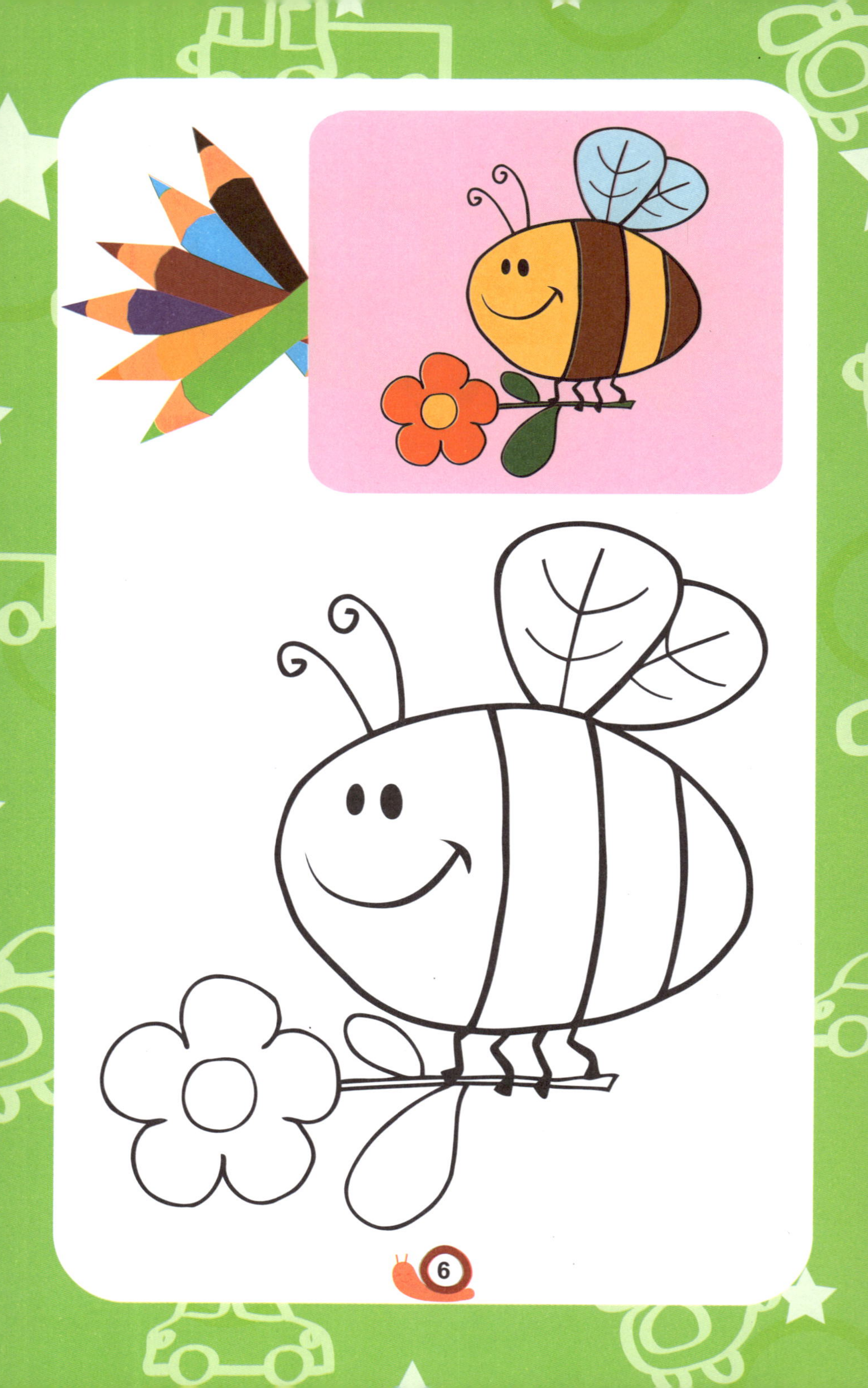

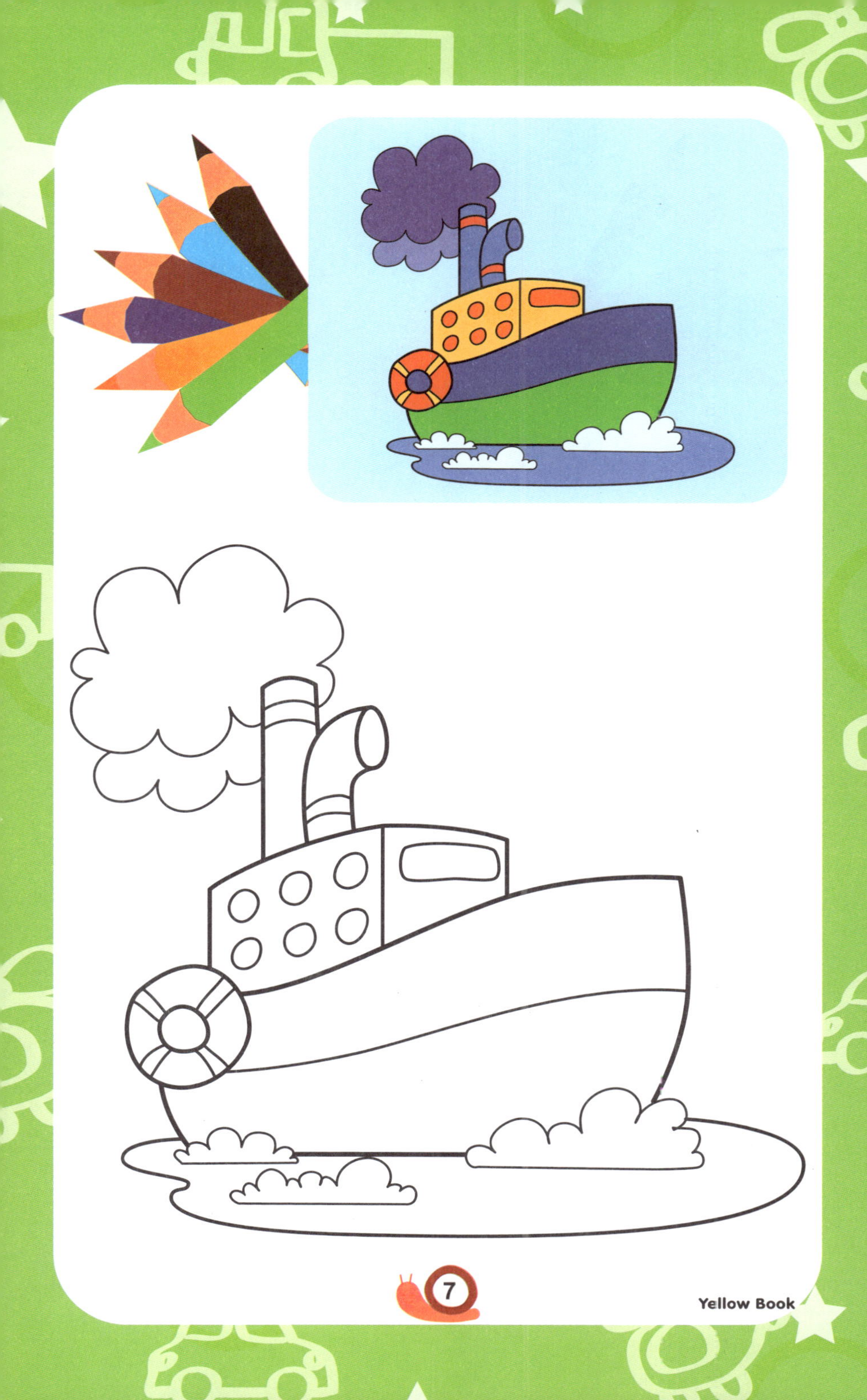

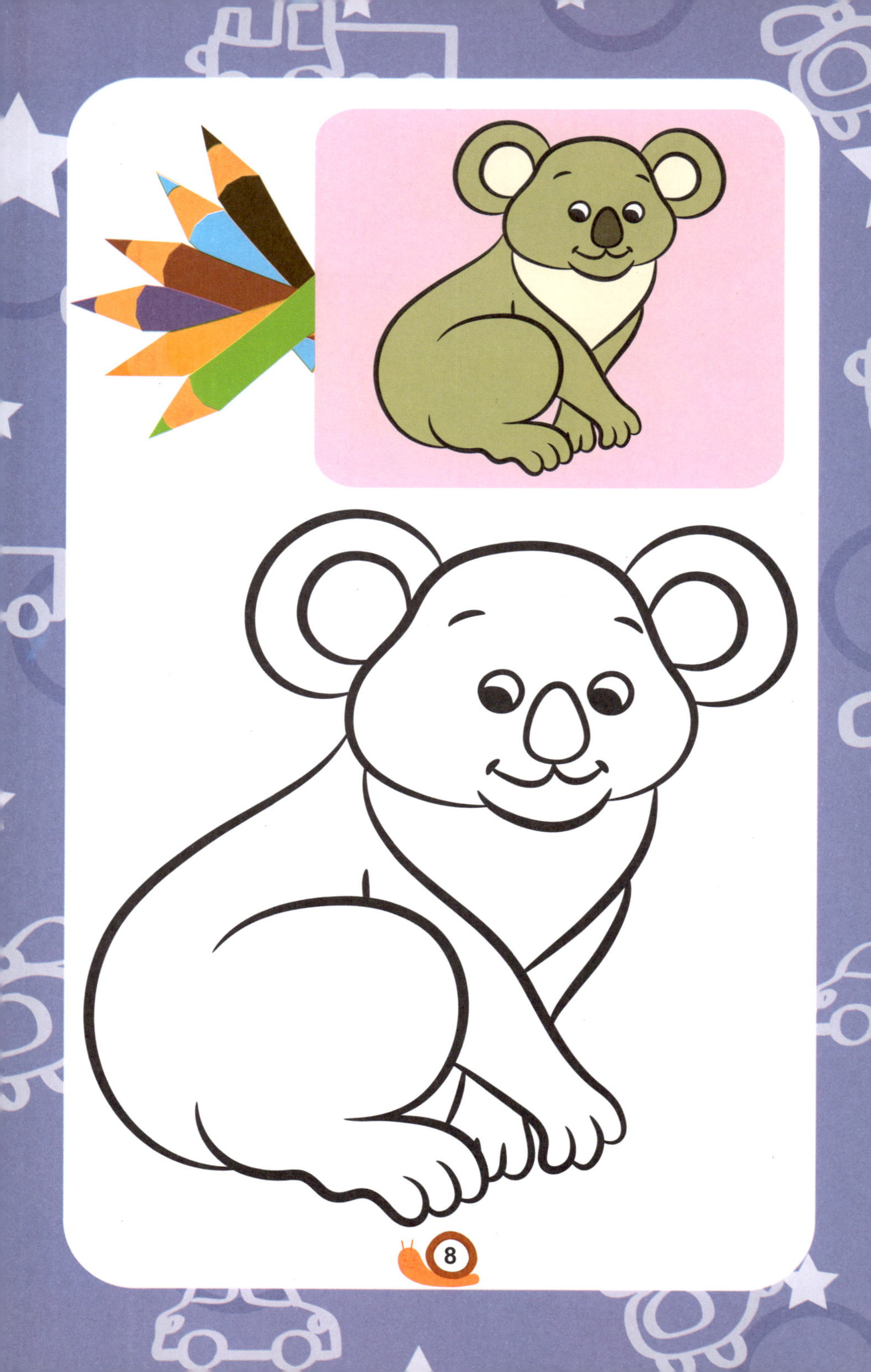

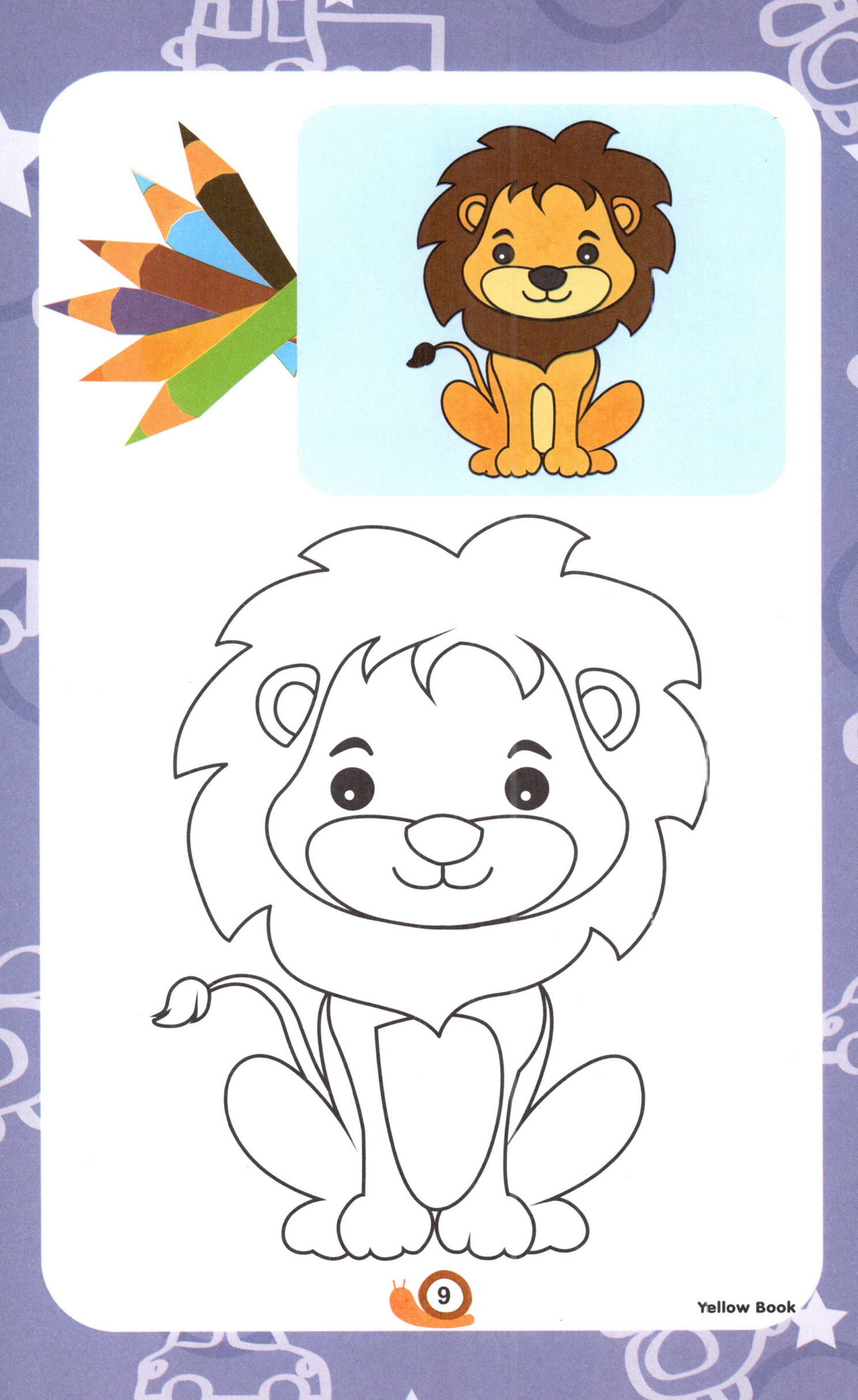

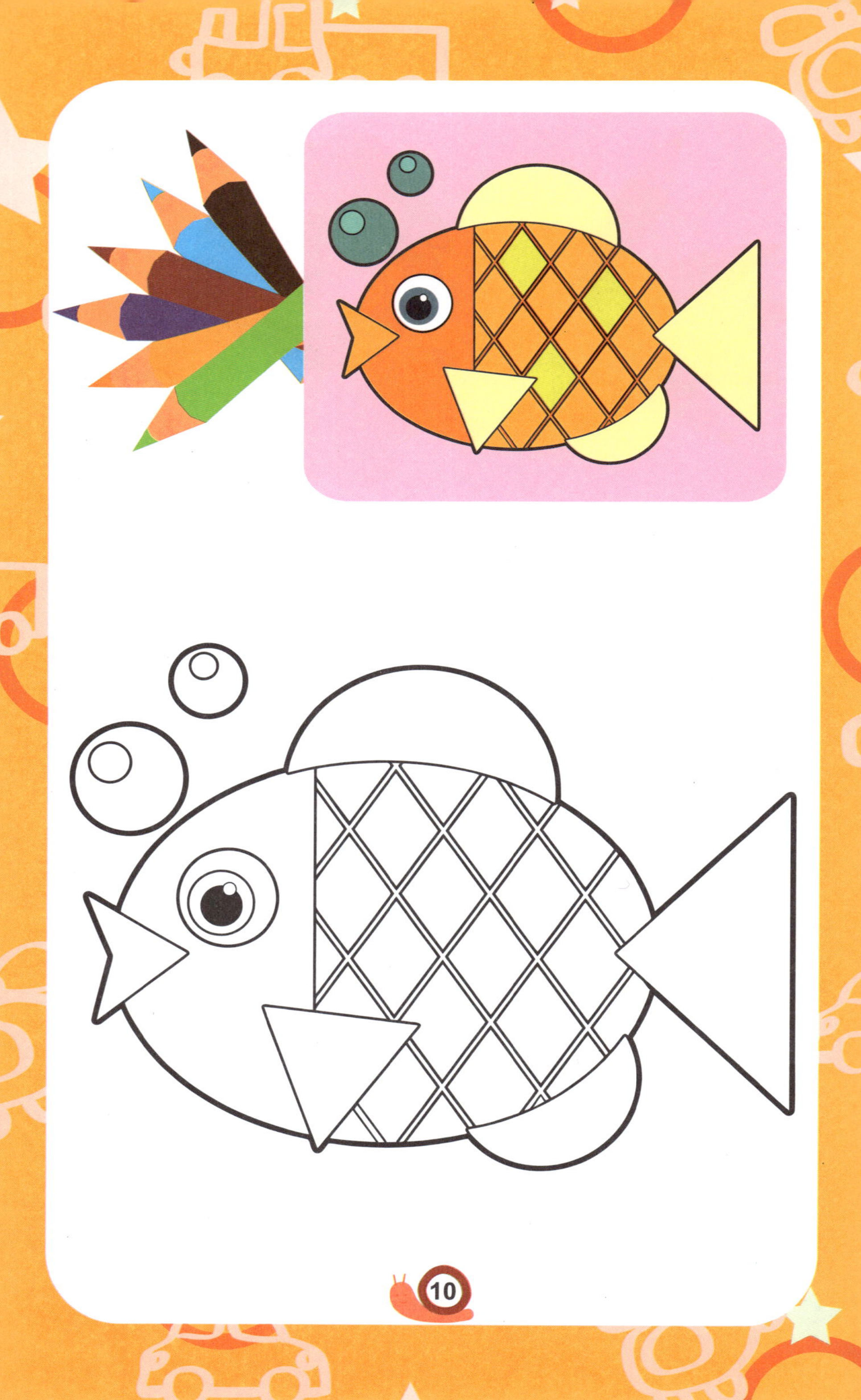

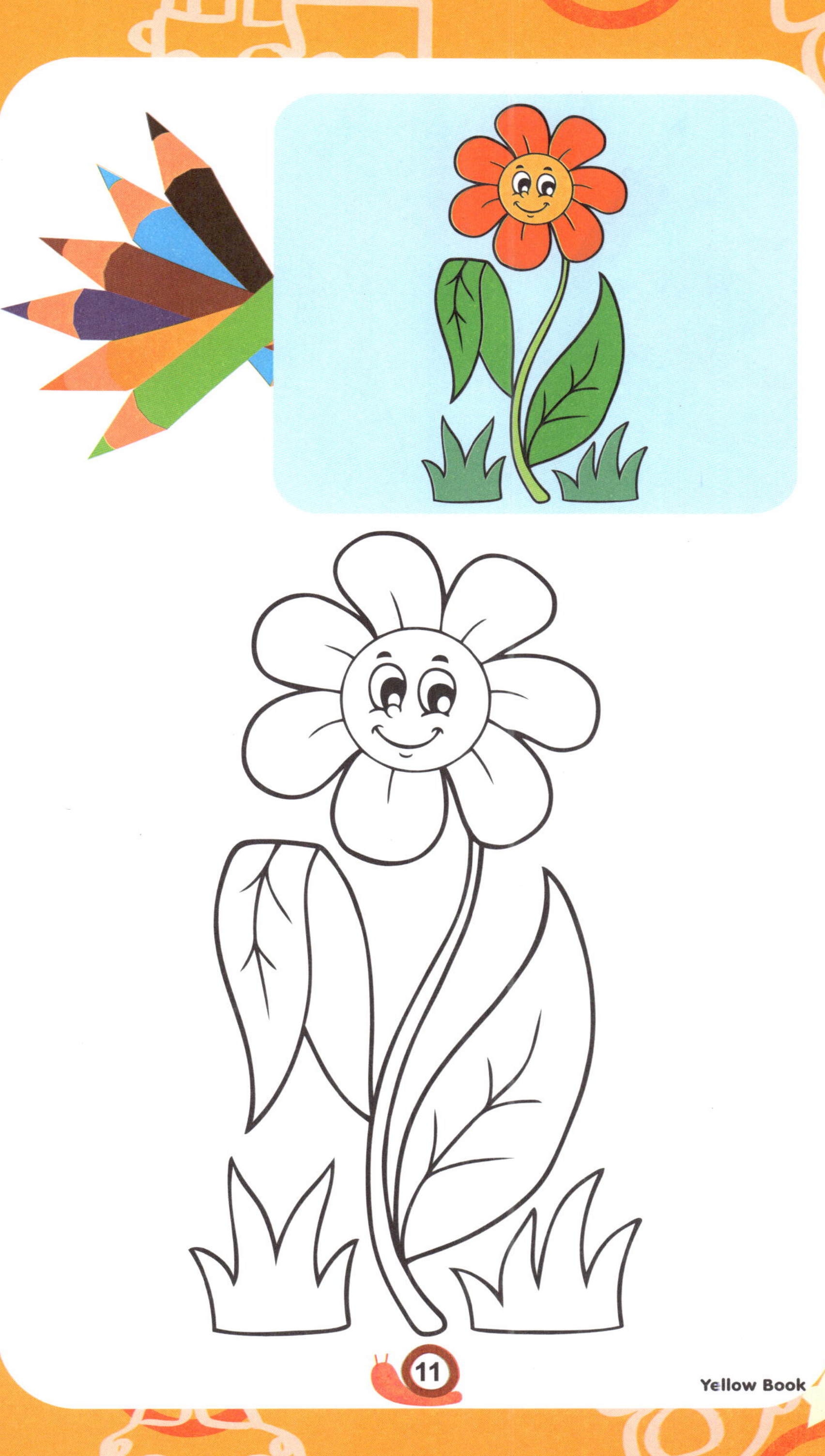

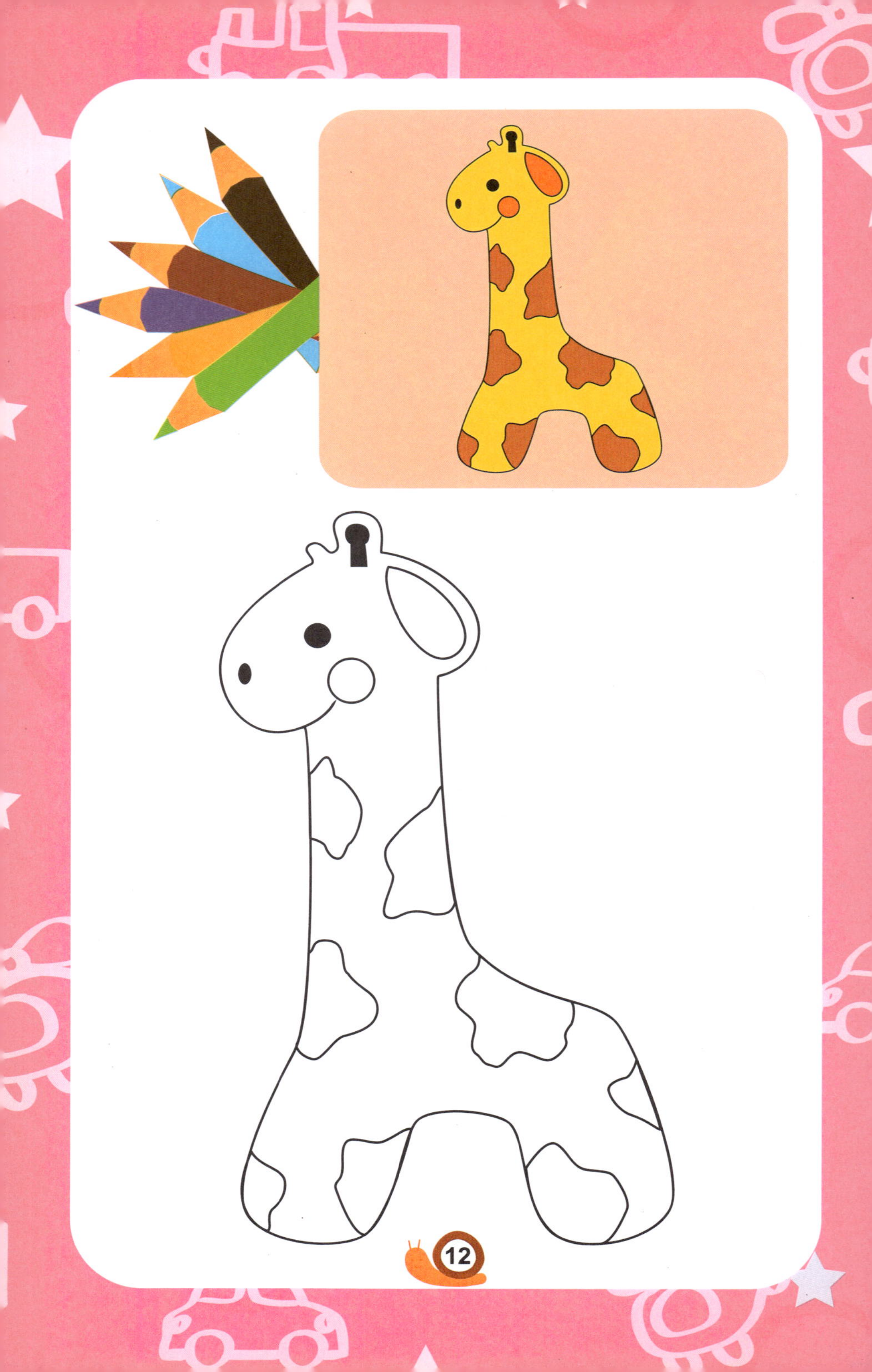

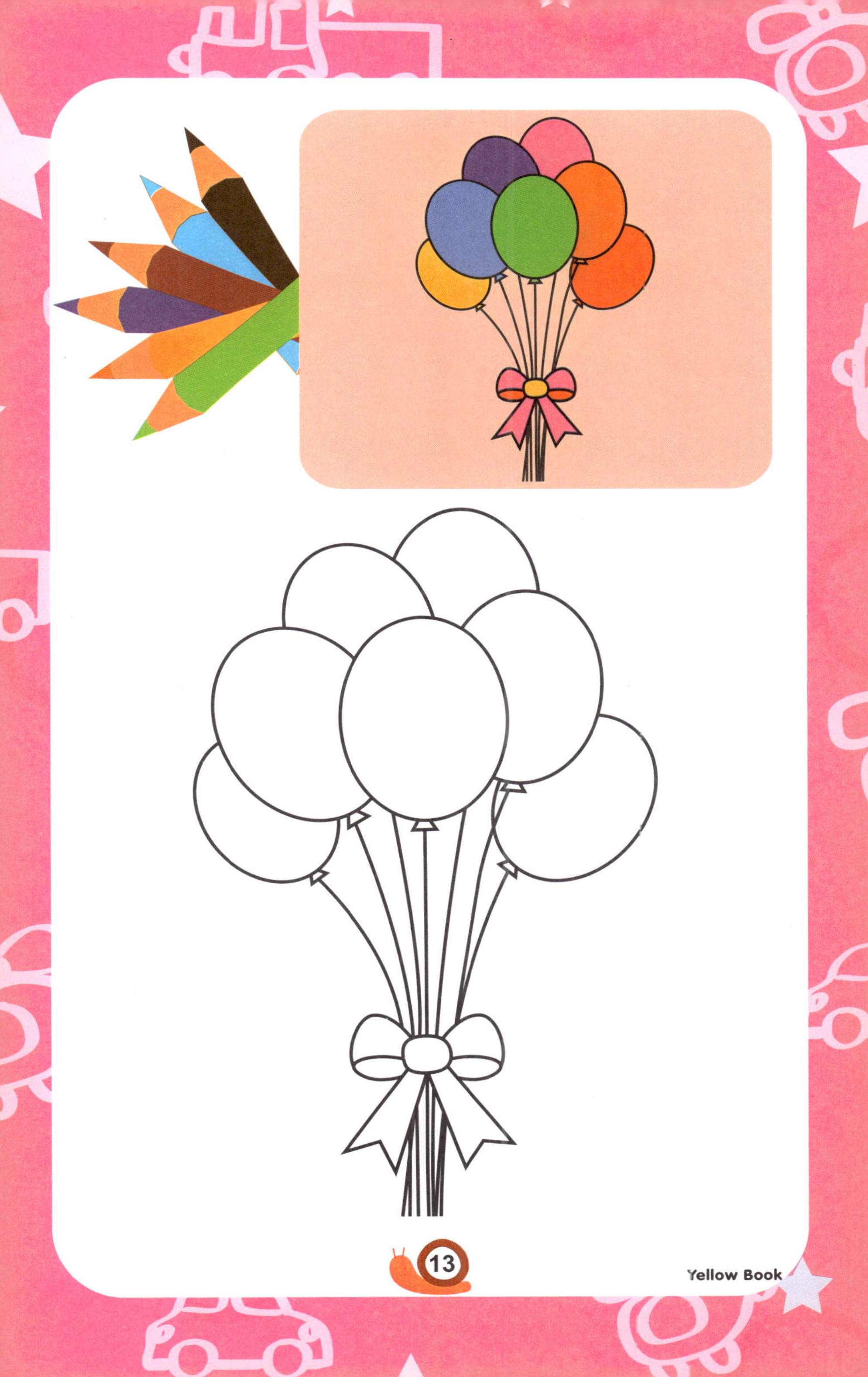

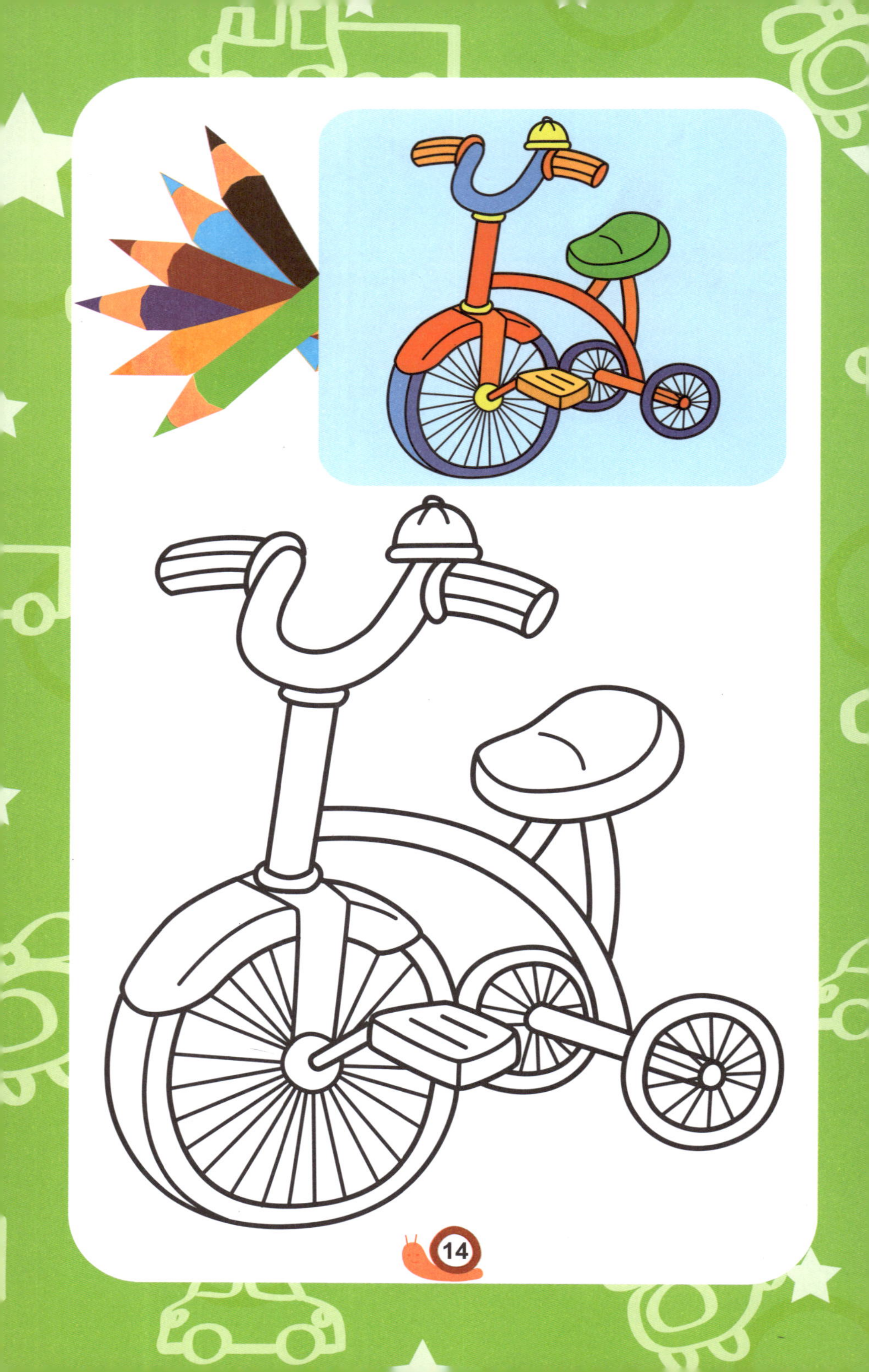

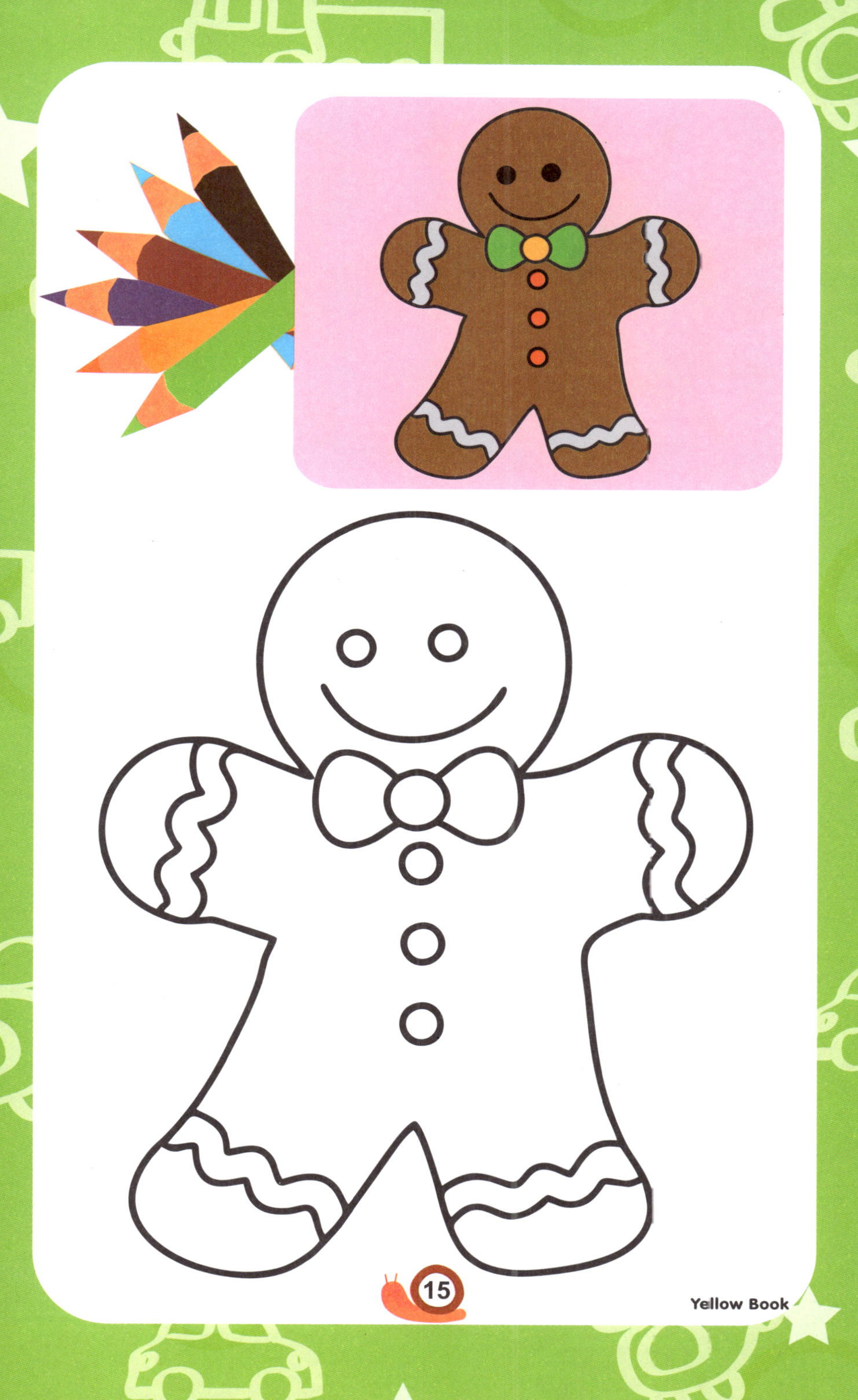

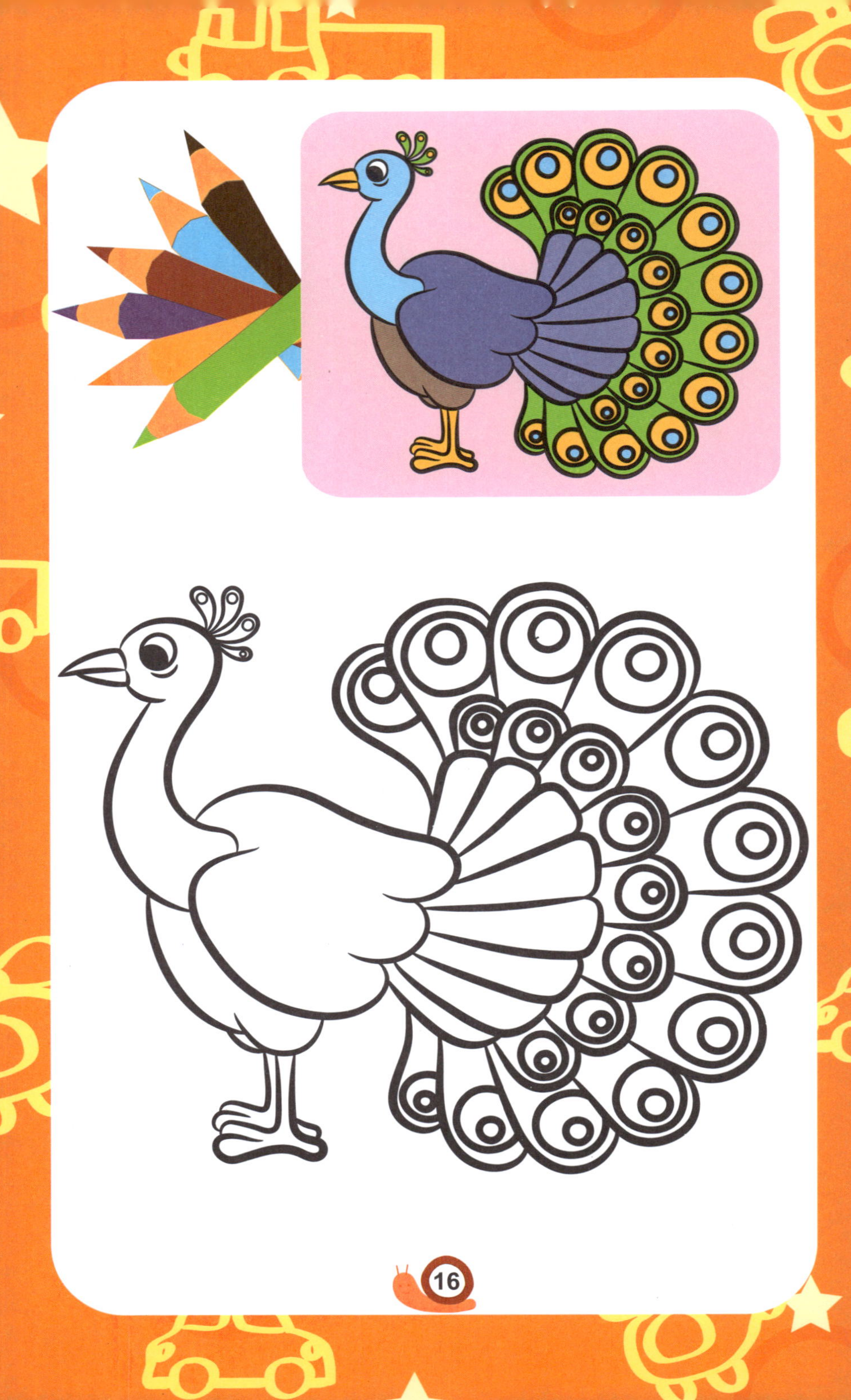